# The Sh
# To Buddnism:

*A Beginners Guide to Understanding Buddhism, Buddhist Teachings and the Life of the Buddha*

Knowledge in Minutes

2

Respective authors own all copyrights not held by the publisher.

The information herein is offered for informational purposes solely,and is universal as so. The presentation of the information is without contract or any type of guarantee assurance.

The trademarks that are used are without any consent, and the publication of the trademark is without permission or backing by the trademark owner. All trademarks and brands within this book are for clarifying purposes only and are the owned by the owners themselves, not affiliated with this document.

## Errors and Feedback

## Please Contact Us If You Find Any Errors

While every effort is taken to ensure the quality and accuracy of this book. Spelling, grammar and other errors are often missed in the early versions of publication.

We appreciate you contacting us first if you noticed any errors in this book before taking any other action.

If you find any issues or errors with this book, please contact us and we'll correct these as soon as possible.
Readers that notify us of errors will be invited to receive advance reader copies of future books published.
**Errors:** errors@wisefoxpub.com

## Feedback

For any general feedback about the book, please feel free to contact us at the email address below:
**Feedback:** feedback@wisefoxpub.com

**Table of Contents**

# Free Bonus Guides on Meditation and Mindfulness

Get 3 free bonus guides to help you incorporate meditation and mindfulness into every day.

**Guide 1: The Power of Meditation**
Learn more about the power of meditation and how it can help you in your personal and professional life.

**Guide 2: Stress Less**
A guide to help reduce stress at home and work with meditation and mindfulness

**Guide 3: The End to Multitasking:**
Learn how to get more done each day by avoiding multi-tasking and being more focused. This is a practical guide for work or study that includes focus exercises to improve mindfulness and increase focus and concentration.

www.wisefoxbooks.com/mindfulguide

**Reviews**

If you enjoy this book, it would be greatly appreciated if you were able to take a few moments to share your opinion and post a review on after you finish reading it.

Even a few words and a rating can be a great help.

**Feedback**
If you don't enjoy the book or have any feedback, please let us know what you didn't enjoy by emailing feedback@wisefoxpub.com

We welcome all comments as they help improve the book based on your feedback.

# Introduction

I want to start by offering my congratulations and thanks to you for purchasing this book! After my long research into the philosophy of Buddhism, I am ecstatic to share what I have learned with you. This book offers an extensive look at Buddhism: its inception, the different forms that have gained popularity over time, and its teachings.

Buddhism offers an end to suffering. Suffering is a broad concept and is not necessarily as dramatic as the word sounds. It can simply be unhappiness, desire for something new in life, boredom, or just being generally dissatisfied with life.

Buddhism does not require you to renounce whatever God or Gods you believe in to reach enlightenment. It is not necessarily a religion; it can also be considered a philosophy or a way of life—even Catholic nuns and Christian priests can practice Buddhism. Buddhism accepts all people; it has no quarrel with other religions, philosophies, or the like.

Buddhism simply offers an understanding and a release from suffering. "Release from suffering" sounds final and almost threatening without a true understanding of the Buddhist meaning for the word. This book can give you an end to suffering that lets you live a long, happy, and healthy life after reaching enlightenment. The Buddha himself lived for over forty years after reaching enlightenment and he died a very happy old man.

If you find yourself dissatisfied with life, this book will teach you about the Buddhist way to free yourself from suffering. You'll find the truth behind why you are unsatisfied and unhappy, and learn the path to enlightenment. This path is easy to follow and asks nothing more from you than to live a good life and reflect on the teachings of the Buddha. You will be able to live life to its fullest potential after reading this book.

This book breaks down Buddhism to its most understandable form and will create an interest that I promise you will want to satisfy. Buddhism is a rich philosophy that will challenge your understanding of the world as you know it.

You will learn why the Buddha turned away from his luxurious life in a palace as a prince and chose to live a much happier existence as a teacher dedicated to relieving the world from its pain.

Read on if you want to discover the Buddha's wisdom and understand the root of unhappiness and how to overcome it.

# Chapter One: Introduction To Buddhism

Buddhism is commonly referred to as a religion, and this can be true, but a better description is that Buddhism is a philosophy. It was founded by Siddhartha Gautama in mid-500 BCE. He was a prince in India whose parents sheltered him from the pain and suffering that went on outside the palace walls. Siddhartha got bored and went outside, and when he saw the suffering of man, he could not in good conscience return to his lavish lifestyle in the palace. He went to study religion in search of the reason for and the end to suffering. Although he searched far and wide, he did not find what he was looking for. He left the religious group that he was studying with and went to meditate and reflect on life. While meditating, he realized enlightenment, Buddhism was born, and Siddhartha Gautama was thereafter known as the Buddha.

Buddhism heavily relies on meditation as a means to reach enlightenment. The core desire of the philosophy is to relieve suffering. In order to do this, one must break the cycle of life, death, and rebirth, known as samsara, in order to reach nirvana. Buddhists believe that they are stuck in this cycle until they reach enlightenment and are finally free from the suffering of life. This is not to say that someone who reaches enlightenment must be dead; they are simply unbothered by the suffering of life. They are in nirvana, which is a state of being, not an actual place. It is a state of being that is free from the confines of suffering. Samsara (the cycle of life, death, and rebirth) is informed by karma. Karma refers to the actions of your past life; the better the actions, the better the life you are reincarnated in, and the worse the actions, the worse the life.

The philosophy can appear dark from uninformed points of view. It preaches that life is suffering and that true happiness is not possible unless you relinquish your concept of what self is. This sounds scary, but with deeper insight, it does not mean what it seems to. Buddhism also always offers hope. Its very core is hope for a better world, a better future, and freedom from suffering for all. It's a desire to end suffering for everyone, all-inclusive. It is not just something pretty to recite and not actually practice. Anyone can practice Buddhism and practice it successfully if their intentions are pure and strong enough.

To attain enlightenment, one must follow the teachings of the Buddha, which include Three Universal Truths, Four Noble Truths, and an Eightfold Path, but before we cover those teachings, we must truly know who the Buddha is. He remains a mystery to a lot of people today. He is often mistaken for a god, just like Buddhism is often mistaken for a religion. Before we can understand his teachings, we need to clear up these misconceptions about the man himself.

# Chapter Two: Who Is The Buddha?

Many people have the wrong perception of the Buddha. They picture a smiling, chubby cross-legged statue, and assume that Buddhists look to the Buddha as a god. These are all fair assumptions based on how the Buddha is depicted in popular media, but they are incorrect. This chapter will shed light on the Buddha and his truth.

## Buddha Is Not A God

Buddha is not considered a god in Buddhism. In fact, the Buddha never claimed to be a god, a messenger of god, or the child of god. He was simply a man and a teacher that reached enlightenment and wanted to spread his wisdom to help others end their own suffering. From the outside looking in, it can appear that Buddha is a god, especially as that is expected from a religion. But in fact, as we have pointed out, Buddhism is not truly a religion; it has been described as a philosophy and as a science. Buddha was a man who lived about 2500 years ago. He was a prince who. after living a life of sheltered luxury, discovered the suffering outside of his palace walls and dedicated the rest of his life to finding a way to end suffering.

# Buddhists Don't Worship Buddha As A God

Buddha is not a god, and he is not worshiped as such. If one travelled to a Buddhist culture, they would see offerings placed at the base of Buddhist statues. Without doing more research or gaining a better understanding of what Buddhism is, it would be easy to assume that these offerings were of worship. Worship is to show reverence or adoration and is typically used in reference to a deity. Buddha is not a deity and his followers do not make offerings out of worship. It would be more accurate to say that Buddhists are making offerings out of respect and out of thankfulness for the Buddha.

## Buddha Is A Teacher

When Buddha became aware of suffering, he set off to try and discover the key to happiness. After years of studying with great religious leaders and meditating, he came to enlightenment. The Buddha then dedicated the rest of his life to travelling and teaching his dedicated followers the way to enlightenment. Buddhism is often referred to as a science or an education system and Buddha was the first great teacher. A Buddha, or someone who becomes enlightened, traditionally becomes a teacher and tries to help others reach enlightenment, as well.

## Buddha Is The Enlightened One

The Buddha was not always the enlightened one, before he
became enlightened he was simply a man named Siddhartha
Gautama. Buddha literally translates to "the awakened one." In
Buddhist beliefs, one day during his studies, Siddhartha
Gautama became absorbed in his meditation and became
enlightened. This meant that he ended the cycle of life, death,
and rebirth that the philosophy of Buddhism believes
inherently leads to suffering. The overarching goal of
Buddhism is to reach enlightenment, and when the Buddha
began his teachings, he sought to help others end that cycle and
thus end their suffering. In Buddhism, there is the Buddha, but
there are many Buddhas, because Buddha simply means
"awakened one." Any Buddhist who reaches enlightenment is a
Buddha.

## Buddha Is Not The Fat Statue

Buddha is often mistakenly depicted as a fat, jolly-looking man
seated in a cross-legged position. He was first depicted this
way in China, where being overweight signified wealth and
good fortune. The fat statue was probably also not even a
depiction of the Buddha originally, but a depiction of the
Chinese deity, Budai. Presenting the Buddha as a fat man does
not really make sense as Buddhism teaches the way of the
middle, which does not allow for one to have the excess food
that would make them overweight.

This should have dispelled some common misconceptions that people have about the Buddha. The next chapter will explore the life of Siddhartha Gautama before he became the Buddha and his journey to becoming the Buddha.

# Chapter Three: The Life Of The Buddha

Before he became the Buddha, he was simply a man, a prince who came from wealth and lived a sheltered life. Once he left his sheltered life, he saw how much suffering happened beyond his palace walls and this motivated him to search for a way to end pain and suffering. Much of what we know about the Buddha is not exactly biography, but more legend, and the narrative has changed over time. However, it is accepted that Buddha really existed by most historians.

## Prince

Siddhartha Gautama was a prince who was born in what is known today as Nepal. He was born in the fifth or sixth century BCE. His mother died shortly after he was born, and his aunt, who was also his father's second wife, took care of him as her own. She would later become the first Buddhist nun. He was raised in seclusion and shielded from religion, suffering, and pain. It was foretold when he was young that he would become either a great military power or a spiritual leader. His father hoped for the former. He believed that sheltering him from things that could make him question the meaning of life would keep him from the path of religion. At 16, Siddhartha was married to his cousin in an arranged marriage, and not long after he married, his wife gave birth to their son.

## The Four Sights

At 29 years old, Siddhartha, who had been kept in luxury in the palace his entire life, wanted to see more of the world. Sources vary on whether he had four visions or went on four journeys outside the palace. Either way, the prince saw four things that shocked him and led to his fateful decision to leave his life behind and search for an end to suffering. He saw an old man, a sick man, and a corpse. When confronted with these sights, he was reasonably upset by them after being sheltered from such harsh realities his entire life. Finally, he saw an ascetic, a wanderer who practiced abstention in an attempt to find eternal peace.

## Searching For Meaning

After witnessing The Four Sights, Siddhartha tried to return to his normal life, but he could take no pleasure in it, knowing what pain and suffering was taking place outside his palace walls. The prince gave up his life of luxury and traded it for the life of a beggar, in a search for enlightenment. He started by seeking the teachings of renowned religious leaders. From them, he learned how to meditate and was taught many different religious philosophies. He was dissatisfied with the teachings, as none of them offered him the reason behind suffering and a solution to end it, which was what he was searching for.

## Giving Up Food

In his search for meaning, he joined a group of companions with like minds to himself. With them, he studied meditation, but they also practiced severe self-discipline. They would hold their breath for a long time, make themselves endure pain, and fast intensely. It is said that the Buddha fasted for nearly six years. Some sources say he survived on only a spoonful of soup a day, while others say that he only ate a few grains of rice.

## The Middle Way

From practicing these two extremes, Siddhartha came to the realization that neither would lead to enlightenment. He grew up in extreme luxury and then fasted for six years before rejecting both ways of life. He believed that the best way to reach nirvana was to pursue a middle way, a way of life that was defined by moderation. Siddhartha wanted people to follow a path of balance. He believed that the way to enlightenment required nourishment to help discipline the mind. When he accepted a bowl of rice, his companions deserted him, believing that he had given up the life of an ascetic.

## Enlightenment

Buddha gained enlightenment underneath the Bodhi Tree. He went into a deep meditation. The trepidation his mind went through while in meditation was a battle with Mara, a demon that Siddhartha had to defeat before reaching enlightenment. Mara claimed that enlightenment belonged to him, but the earth itself is said to bear witness to enlightenment belonging to Siddhartha. In his meditation, he came to realize his past incarnations, being able to remember them in detail, and he could see how the good and the bad deeds committed by past reincarnations had a direct effect on the nature of his next life. He awoke from his meditation enlightened, becoming the Buddha.

The Buddha was first reluctant to teach, as he was unsure how to teach what he had learned. It was something that needed to be experienced and could not be taught. Although he was unsure at first, he did teach the way of the Buddha. There are even Buddhas who have chosen to continue their cycle of life, death, and rebirth in order to continue teaching and aiding followers of the Buddhist philosophy. His teachings are still practiced today and have split into many different schools of Buddhism.

# Chapter Four: Schools Of Buddhism

Buddhism has been practiced for thousands of years, and like any philosophy, there are different ways to interpret the teachings of the Buddha. Over the course of time, these different interpretations became validated and grew into different branches, or schools, of Buddhism. All fall under the overarching philosophy of following the teachings of the Buddha, but each go about it differently. This chapter will explore the main schools of Buddhism.

## Theravada

Theravada Buddhists believe that they follow the words of the elder Buddhas most closely. There is the Buddha (Siddhartha Gautama), and then subsequent elder Buddhas after him. Theravada Buddhists reject supernatural beings. They do not worship idols or believe that they need the aid of a god to gain enlightenment. This form of Buddhism emphasizes that one can only rely on themselves to reach enlightenment. In fact, the only way for them to reach enlightenment is through themselves. Theravada Buddhists abstain from all things evil. They believe that any evil they put into the world will affect them in their reincarnated life negatively. An emphasis is placed on monastic living, but a layperson can be a follower, as well. There is no exclusion in Buddhism, as any person can follow the teachings of the Buddha. Like most forms of Buddhism, there is an emphasis placed on meditation and concentration.

Monastic life is the ideal way of life for Theravada Buddhists. The Theravada way of Buddhism is best as a full-time occupation. Some monastic communities have members that join as young as seven, but anyone can join at any age. A novice monk is referred to as a samanera, while a full monk is a bikkhu. Every monk and nun subscribe to the five precepts of Buddhism, which will be explained in depth later in the book.

In Theravada Buddhism, monks and nuns are required to follow the training of the monastic order, which is called the Vinaya. The Vinaya consists of 227 rules for monks and even more for nuns.

Theravada Buddhism has two forms of meditation: calming meditation and insight meditation. The former is called samatha meditation and the latter is vipassana meditation. Samatha meditation is the oldest type of meditation. This type of meditation makes the meditator calmer, allowing the mind to reach higher states of consciousness. Vipassana meditation attempts to make the meditator aware of the true nature of things. This understanding must be free from preconceived notions and opinions that influence and change a person's perception of the true nature of the world.

# Mahayana

Mahayana Buddhism is a group of Buddhist traditions, not a form of Buddhism on its own. It's a title for Buddhist traditions that encompasses Pure Land, Zen, and Tibetan Buddhism. These forms of Buddhism are all searching for a way to break the cycle of life, death, and rebirth by reaching nirvana. The Buddha was able to break this cycle when he reached enlightenment. Mahayana Buddhists follow the way of the bodhisattva. The bodhisattva is a way of life that emphasizes general selflessness and wanting to relieve all others from pain and suffering, as the Buddha began his original journey in order to discover an end to suffering. Mahayana Buddhists actually take the Bodhisattva Vow:

*However innumerable sentient beings are, I vow to save them. However inexhaustible the defilements are, I vow to extinguish them. However immeasurable the dharmas are, I vow to master them. However incomparable enlightenment is, I vow to attain it.*

In this form of Buddhist tradition, Buddha is believed to have three forms: one is his physical form (dharmakaya), the second is his body of enjoyment (sambhogakaya), and the third is his transcendent form (nirmanakaya).

## Tibetan Buddhism

Tibetan Buddhism, once popular, is now an exiled religion since the Chinese occupation of Tibet. Tibetan Buddhism is influenced by older Tibetan religions and because of this, there is a strong supernatural influence in their teachings. Old Tibetan Gods are both revered and feared in Tibetan Buddhism, and Buddhas are viewed as godlike. This is very contradictory to the other forms of Buddhism commonly practiced. There is a strong reliance on the visual, using art and graphics to make the practice more accessible. Tibetan Buddhists perform rituals that are bright, colorful, and that often involve chants and musical elements. They place an emphasis on death and dying in order to truly value living.

In the United Kingdom, there is a version of Tibetan Buddhism gaining popularity called the New Kadampa Tradition. This is considered to be outside of Buddhist traditions. Although referred to as New, it was founded in the eleventh century. New Kadampa Tradition was founded as a reintroduction of Buddhism to Tibet. Buddhism had been introduced two hundred years prior, but it was almost completely forgotten due to anti-Buddhist purges that came about during the time period where Tibet was transitioning from a large religious following of Bon (the traditional Tibetan religion) to more people following Buddhism. This form of Buddhism is praised for its accessibility to everyone and emphasizes the combination and harmony of the Sutra and the Tantra. This is largely thanks to Je Tsongkharpa, a Tibetan Buddhist Saint who added clearer meanings to the sacred Buddhist texts.

## The Dalai Lama

Lamas are teachers in Tibetan Buddhism, and many of them are reincarnations of past Lamas. The Dalai Lama is the head monk and was traditionally in charge of governing Tibet. After the Chinese occupation of Tibet in 1959, that is no longer accurate, as they exiled Tibetan Buddhism. The word Dalai literally translates as "depth," referring to the depth of the wisdom that the Dalai Lama possesses.

The concept of a Dalai Lama can seem contradictory to the philosophy of Buddhism. The Dalai Lama is in a constant state of reincarnation. In Buddhism, the most revered people are those who have reached enlightenment, and once reaching enlightenment, the samsara cycle ends. How can the Dalai Lama have reached enlightenment and still be in the cycle of life, death, and rebirth?

The Dalai Lama is a tulku. This term refers to someone who has chosen to be continually reincarnated. Tulkus believe that they have work to do that is more important than ending the cycle of life, death, and rebirth for themselves.

There have only been fourteen Dalai Lamas in the entire history of Buddhism. The first two Dalai Lamas were given the title after their deaths. Tenzin Gyatso is the current Dalai Lama. After the death of the Dalai Lama, high ranking Lamas search for a boy born around the same time as the death, believing that they will be the incarnation of the past Dalai Lama. High Lamas have methods of ensuring that a child is truly the reincarnation of the Dalai Lama. They may have a dream about a location, or a mark that will identify the boy. If the Dalai Lama is cremated, they will watch the direction the smoke blows and follow that. They can also go the Lhamo Lhatso, which is a holy lake in Tibet. The High Lama will look into the lake for a sign that tells them where to search for the new Dalai Lama. Tenzin Gyatso was identified through a vision that came to the lake. The High Lamas will then present the found boy artifacts, and among the objects there are some that belonged to the previous Dalai Lama. If the boy chooses the artifacts that belonged to the Dalai Lama, the boy is proven to be the Dalai Lama's reincarnation. The current Dalai Lama does not believe that he will be reincarnated, and if he is reborn, he believes that it will not be in Tibet or any other country under oppression.

## Chinese Chan Buddhism / Japanese Zen Buddhism

Chinese Chan Buddhism is commonly referred to as Zen Buddhism, which is the Japanese word for Chan. The two, Chan and Zen, are mostly identical. Zen just happened to be the title that became most well-known to western civilization. The word literally translates to "meditation"—which is the utmost emphasis of this form of Buddhism. For ease of reading, I will refer to both Chinese Chan Buddhism and Japanese Zen Buddhism as Zen Buddhism. Zen Buddhism was solidified as a form of Buddhism nearly a thousand years after Buddhism was created. Zen Buddhism was widely practiced in China and eventually Japan. Bodhidharma is the founding father of Zen Buddhism and is said to have arrived in China in 520 C.E., wanting to spread Buddhism. Zen focuses almost entirely on meditation as a means to discover enlightenment.

Zen Buddhism seeks to teach enlightenment through the recognition that one is already enlightened.

The emphasis on one's self sets Zen Buddhism apart from traditional Buddhism. This is also the reason why writings are not as significant to Zen Buddhism as they are to other forms of Buddhism. All forms of Buddhism utilize meditation as an important tool to reaching enlightenment, but no other form holds it in as high esteem as Zen Buddhism.

The specific form of meditation practiced by Zen Buddhists is called Zazen. This means sitting meditation. In order to practice Zazen, you must find a room that is a neutral temperature where you can attain complete concentration and where you will not be bothered. Zazen is practiced in the full or half lotus position—each leg over the opposite knee—seated on a round cushion. The round cushion is called a zafu. Beneath the zafu, a blanket called a zabuton should be laid down. This is meant to help cushion the knees as they rest on the ground in the lotus position. Zazen requires that you maintain good posture and keep your eyes open. Meditation is typically shown with the meditator having closed eyes, but this is an incorrect depiction. The eyes must remain open in order to avoid day dreaming and becoming sleepy.
Zen is indescribable. It's a practice, something that needs to be experienced in order to be understood. Trying to describe Zen to someone is like trying to explain the beauty of a full moon to a person who has never seen it. You can paint a pretty picture for them, but words will never match what it is like to physically experience the sight of a full moon.

## Pure Land Buddhism

This form of Buddhism is popular because it doesn't require its followers to be knowledgeable or monks. It relies on the belief in the Pure Land and the reverence of Amitabha Buddha. Its followers must call upon Amitabha Buddha for help and if devout, they will be reborn in the Pure Land. What makes this facet of Buddhism so unique is that its overarching goal is to reach the Pure Land, not to reach nirvana. The Pure Land is a

place free from distractions where they can work towards
nirvana in peace.

The story of Amitabha Buddha is that he was once a king and after seeing too much suffering, he became a monk. He wanted to become a Buddha to create a Pure Land and in his vows, he stated that those who recite his name will be reborn into the Pure Land. As a result, Pure Land Buddhism is heavily reliant on the practice of chanting Amitabha Buddha's name.

There are two sects to Pure Land Buddhism. The first was created by Honen Shonin, called Jodo Shu. The focus of Jodu Shu was the Nembutsu. This is the act of sincere and focused chanting, the same chant that Pure Land Buddhism emphasizes for Amitabha. Honen is said to have recited the Nembutsu sixty thousand times a day. He attracted a large following, of all classes of people. This resulted in him being exiled to a remote part of Japan. The Shin Sect was created by Shinran Shonin who was a monk that broke his vows by getting married. This sect is also known as Jodo Shinshu. He believed in the Nembutsu, but placed more emphasis on the faith you place behind the words you are reciting.
These two sects of Buddhism are the most popularly practiced forms, even more popular than Zen Buddhism.

## Difference Between Theravada and Mahayana

Theravada Buddhism is a form of Buddhism, and Mahayana is an umbrella description for some forms of Buddhism. A lot of light can be shed on their differences just by the meanings of the words—Mahayana means "great vehicle" and Theravada means "teaching of the elders." Mahayana Buddhists believe that the only way to achieve enlightenment is to become a Buddha, while in Theravada Buddhism, they do not require an enlightened one to be a Buddha. One can become enlightened, but does not need to become a teacher to aid others to enlightenment. Mahayana Buddhism emphasizes meditation and offerings, while Theravada places the highest importance on meditation, but also emphasizes donations and morality. Theravada requires its followers to find enlightenment by following the eightfold path. Mahayana uses the bodhisattva to reach enlightenment. Although these appear very different on the surface, all forms of Buddhism when looked at closely enough are very similar and only want their followers to be free from suffering and aid others in freeing themselves from suffering.

## Difference Between Zen Buddhism and Other Forms of Buddhism

All other forms of Buddhism have an element of meditation, but none are more reliant on its practice than Zen Buddhism. Zen Buddhists believe that the only way to gain enlightenment is through mediation and through releasing one's mind from the confines of the world and worldly problems. Enlightenment can be reached at any time, almost at random. Buddhists strive to achieve enlightenment, which they believe will lead them to nirvana and break them out of the life, death, and rebirth cycle.

Writings are not of as much significance to Zen Buddhism as to other forms. The scriptures that are used in Zen Buddhism are stories and riddles called koans. The purpose of them is to break the student free from logical thought.

The main difference between Zen Buddhism and other form of Buddhism is how internalized the philosophy is. Buddhism and its many other forms tend to emphasize sympathy and kindness towards the outside world. For these forms of Buddhism, the ultimate way to reach nirvana is to aid in the creation of a better world by helping others. Zen Buddhists believe in a more internal struggle to reach enlightenment.

This section brought to light the differences between the many forms of Buddhism that coexist in the world today. The beauty of Buddhism is that these can all exist without issue because it is a philosophy and can be interpreted in so many different ways. Buddhism is entirely non-discriminatory, even within its own varying practices. The only requirement is to spread the teachings of how to end suffering.

# Chapter Five: Teachings Of The Buddha

The Buddha himself described his teachings as understanding suffering and putting an end to it. The collective teachings of Buddha are called the Dharma or the Dhammapada, where the former refers to the general teachings and the latter refers to a textual collection of those teachings.

## The Dharma/The Dhammapada

The Dharma, in its simplest form, is the term used for the teachings of the Buddha, but it really means much more than that. A more accurate interpretation would be that Dharma is what holds the natural universe together. It is the second of the Three Jewels of Buddhism, the other two being the Buddha and the Sangha. The Buddha, on his death bed, gave sage advice on how to continue his teachings, known as the four reliances: "Rely on the teaching, not on the person; Rely on the meaning, not on the words; Rely on the definitive meaning, not on the provisional; Rely on your wisdom mind, not on your ordinary mind."

The Dharma has different meanings in Theravada Buddhism and Mahayana Buddhism. In Mahayana Buddhism, the word Dharma refers to both the teachings and enlightenment simultaneously. In Theravada, Dharma also refers to more than just the doctrines of the Buddha: It refers to the doctrines themselves, the practice of the doctrines, and the attainment of enlightenment. Later, the Dharma was interpreted as fourfold—the world as it is, the laws of nature, the duties given by the laws of nature, and the end result of preforming these duties. It has also been said to have six characteristics:

1. It was taught by the Buddha.
2. It can be realized through internal efforts.
3. It is both without time and present in every moment.

4. It does not have to be accepted on blind faith, it can be vetted.
5. It leads to entrance into nirvana.
6. It can only be known through insight.

Both Theravada and Mahayana Buddhism refer to the Dharma Body or the truth body. In Theravada, a Buddha is understood to be the physical embodiment of the Dharma. This is also true in Mahayana Buddhism, but they believe that a Buddha has three forms, one of these being the dharmakaya, which is the unification of all beings and things.

The Dharma is the overarching teachings of the Buddha. The specific teachings will be discussed in the following chapters.

# Chapter Six: The Three Universal Truths

Buddhism offers three universal truths. These, in appearance, seem to be nihilistic and harsh, but Buddhists do not view them as such. They believe that by understanding these truths fully, they can lead truly happy lives, something they would not have without these truths.

## Anicca

Anicca is the truth that everything changes constantly and everything is dependent on something else. This applies to the smallest atoms and the largest mountains, even feelings and thoughts are in constant fluctuation. Things that appear to stay the same are simply being replaced with something similar—like a stream of water: it's never the same stream twice, but always appears to be the same.

## Anatta

Anatta is similar to the truth of Anicca, but refers to the impermanence of self. It literally means "no self." Because of the Buddhist truth that everything is impermanent, that means that a person is also constantly changing, therefore the concept of self cannot exist. The process of growing old is also part of this truth. Buddhism accepts that there is a mind and a body, but not a self, at least not in the unchanging understanding of the word.

## Dukkha

Dukkha is the truth of suffering. The Buddha believed that the impermanence of life is what causes suffering, that because everything is changing constantly, we are deprived of true happiness. Dukkha does not refer solely to pain, but to boredom, being uncomfortable, etc.—essentially, Dukkha is everything that is unsatisfactory in life. Buddhism teaches that no one is free from experiencing Dukkha, but offers ways to overcome it.

These Universal Truths are called this because Buddhists believe that they are true for everything in the universe. Only by understanding these truths can one be free from the suffering that they can cause. All of the Buddha's teachings are based on these truths.

# Chapter Seven: The Four Noble Truths

The Buddha's first sermon centered around the foundation of Buddhism, which are the Four Noble Truths. These truths are the very essence of Buddhism. These truths revealed themselves to the Buddha when he was meditating and first became enlightened. The understanding of these truths can lead to enlightenment, and free the person who attains understanding from suffering, which is why they are referred to as noble. These Four Noble truths are part of the Dharma.

## Duhkha – The Truth of Suffering

The first noble truth is that suffering is a part of life. In fact, it can even be interpreted to mean life is suffering. The most obvious examples of Duhkha are the first three of the four sights: old age, sickness, and death. Suffering does not begin and end there, though. Buddha taught that suffering is feeling unfulfilled and being unsatisfied with life. Duhkha's translation, like so many others, is not entirely accurate, and its translation to suffering can make Buddhism seem much darker or more pessimistic than it is. The suffering of life is a truth that one must come to grips with in order to find a solution to the suffering.

## Samudaya – The Origin of Suffering

Before coming to a solution, the Buddha wanted to understand the origin of suffering, where it came from. The reason for suffering is desire or craving something to make one's self happy. According to the universal truths, there is no self, so trying to make one's self happy will inevitably lead to disappointment and dissatisfaction. The problem isn't with the desire itself, but with the attachment we create with the thing through desire, whether that be a thing, person, or idea. We are going to be upset with our desire because even if we attain it, it will inevitably change—because everything is constantly changing.

## Nirodha – The Truth Of An End To Suffering

This truth promises that there is a cure to suffering. Understanding the cause of suffering means that you can put an end to it. If the cause is desire, then the way to end to it would be to stop desiring things. This may sound confusing if you still subscribe to the idea of a self, but through accepting and understanding the second universal truth, you can let go of the attachment you have to your desires. By doing this, you can reach enlightenment and when you eventually die, you can reach nirvana and be released from the cycle of life, death, and rebirth.

## Magga – The Truth Of The Path To End Suffering

This truth refers to the path to end all suffering. This is the Buddha's prescription, if you will, to cure suffering. This is the Eightfold Path. The majority of the Buddha's 45 years teaching was focused on this noble truth. This path is all-encompassing; every aspect of life is discussed and has a point on the path. This path makes the earlier truths more than just theory; it proves these truths and makes them more than just conjecture. This path is also referred to as the Middle Way, which is a completely balanced life, unhindered by excess or desire.

The Middle Way sounds contradictory to modern life. Excess is in fashion, but judging by the Buddha's origin, it always has been. The Buddha taught that the Middle Way was the way to enlightenment.

# Chapter Eight: The Middle Way

The Buddha is hardly the first or the last to preach a middle way of life, one not tainted with extremism on either end of the scale. Aristotle had a similar philosophy, what he called the golden mean, where "every virtue is a mean between two extremes, each of which is a vice." Buddhist traditions state that the Middle Way was the first of Buddha's teachings once he became enlightened. The Middle Way is another umbrella term, and it encompasses the Eightfold Path.

After experiencing such luxury in his youth, living in a palace where his parents shielded him from suffering, Siddhartha Gautama was restless to see what was beyond his palace walls. He found suffering and chose to leave his life of luxury behind to search for a cure to suffering. In his time searching for the cure, he lived the opposite extreme of his child and early adulthood. He was studying with a religious group who practiced self-mortification and starvation. Siddhartha Gautama believed that neither way of life would ever lead to an end to suffering, and that both had hindered his ability to find the answers he was searching for. Giving stock to legend, not long after leaving his life of self-mortification, Siddhartha Gautama meditated for six days and nights under the Bodhai Tree and was awakened.

The Middle Way and the Eightfold Path are interconnected. The Eightfold Path is essentially a guide to living life in the Middle Way.

# Chapter Nine:  The Eightfold Path

In this chapter, you will learn how to live the fourth Noble Truth and the Middle Way. The Eightfold Path can be separated into three qualities: wisdom, morality, and meditation. The Eightfold Path is depicted traditionally as a wheel with eight prongs, because none are more important than the other and each must be followed with the same level of dedication as the next.

## Wisdom

### Right Understanding Or View

The right view or understanding means that you are seeing the world as it truly is. It means you understand the way that suffering and reality are intertwined. Essentially, this path is to understand the Dharma; the Three Universal Truths, the Four Noble Truths, and the concepts of karma and rebirth.

### Right Intention or Thought

You must be doing things for the right reasons, with the correct intentions behind your actions. This can also refer to realizing your true reasons for practicing Buddhism. You cannot be practicing Buddhism for selfish reasons, you must have an unselfish desire to reach enlightenment. This is also a basic rule of doing good and acting on good intentions.

## Morality

### Right Speech

This path is the path of abstaining from defamation, lying, abusive speech, gossiping, and the like. This does not mean you must refrain from sharing opinions and ideas, but that your intentions behind speaking are to do good rather than cause harm.

## Right Action

This means that one must live compassionately and ethically. It means not stealing or killing, as well as not engaging in sexual misconduct or state-altering alcohol and drugs. You must act in a way that is not going to be harmful to yourself or to others.

## Right Livelihood

This path is about how you make your living. Is your job doing more harm than good in the world? Does it have no impact on the world? The original meaning of this had a lot to do with the slaughter of animals for livelihood, but now it can be interpreted as always having honest business dealings and ensuring that your work is not harming any person, being, or thing.

# Meditation

## Right Effort

Without putting proper effort into the Eightfold Path, there is no real path. You have to work hard to follow each step of the path and abstain from all things that are evil. You must also avoid negative thoughts, replace anger with compassion, pride with humbleness, and jealousy with generosity. This also means that you are working towards overcoming the things that create suffering: desire, selfishness, and attachment.

## Right Mindfulness

This is to have a clear understanding of mind and body—how you are feeling mentally and physically. Everything you think, say, and do must be paid attention to. Mindfulness should be in the present, and can help you control the attachment behind desires by reminding you that there is no self. This can also refer to meditation.

## Right Contemplation

Before meditation, one must be free of distractions. Mindfulness and contemplation are intertwined, contemplation being the vehicle through which mindfulness comes. Contemplation is the meditation and mindfulness is the state of mind one must be in for meditation to be useful. It is a tool that can help anchor you to the present.

Walking this path is not easy and it can take a while to fully understand each step. It can require completely changing the way we see the universe and our role within it. This path is the fourth of the Noble Truths; it is the solution, the cure to end suffering. These are not linear steps that one can take to reach enlightenment. You do not have to be a master of one step to go to the next. They must all be practiced simultaneously, as each step supports another.

# Chapter Ten: The Five Precepts

Precepts are vows or promises. All Buddhists make five precepts to the Buddha not to commit certain acts. These are the five core precepts taken by all Buddhists; monks and nuns can take up to 400 precepts. The five precepts can also be known as the Panchasila, which is the Pali word for them.

The purpose of these precepts is to avoid actions that will hurt yourself or others. These may sound similar to the ten commandments, but if broken these do not result in wrath or punishment. One must simply understand and note where the breach has been made and how to avoid it. The consequences of your actions are more reliant on your intentions than the actions themselves, which relates to karma in Buddhist teachings.

## The Five Precepts

1) I undertake to observe the rule to abstain from taking life.
2) I undertake to observe the rule to abstain from taking what is not given.
3) I undertake to observe the rule to abstain from sexual misconduct.
4) I undertake to observe the rule to abstain from false speech.
5) I undertake to observe the rule to abstain from intoxicants.

## Abstaining From Taking Life

This appears to be a basic rule across most philosophies and religions. In Buddhism, it refers to taking or harming any life. There is more stock given to larger animals than smaller, the effort used in the taking of the life is taken into account. Vegetarianism is encouraged in the Buddhist philosophy. This is more than just a rule stating that you won't kill; it is a commitment to a non-violent lifestyle. Killing a human is obviously wrong, but approval of killing others is, as well. Believing that a person should be killed or that it was good that they were killed is breaking this precept.

## Abstaining From Taking What Is Not Given

"To take what is not given" means the taking of that which does not belong to you. You must respect others' property. You do not have a right to something that has not been given to you. This precept does not only refer to tangible things, but also to metaphysical things such as time and effort. You should be careful not to waste another's time and energy when it can be avoided. The basics behind the precept urge the follower to be kind and respectful of others.

## Abstaining From Sexual Misconduct

Buddhism recognizes and accepts sexual desires as a truth of life. Buddhist teachings acknowledge that sexual desires and temptations are sometimes the most difficult obstacle to overcome in reaching enlightenment. Sexual misconduct is forbidden. This does not mean the act of making love or engaging in consensual sex is forbidden. Acts such as adultery and rape are not tolerated. These acts cause harm to others and yourself: physical, mental, and emotional turmoil.

## Abstaining From False Speech

Understanding and respecting the truth is an incredibly important principle of Buddhist teachings. Denial of truth is the same as using false speech. This denial can create confusion and guilt within the mind and body. Denying the truth is not the only form of lying that Buddhists must refrain from. They cannot tell half-truths, white lies, exaggerations, or understatements. They must work toward being completely honest. Through being honest with one's self and the surrounding world, misunderstanding and disharmony can be reduced.

## Abstaining From Intoxicants

Intoxicants, substances that alter your state of mind and consciousness like drugs and alcohol, are not permitted in Buddhism. Buddhist teachings have a high regard for wisdom. Drugs and alcohol can harm a person's wisdom. These intoxicants are also harmful to the health of the consumer. Chances of committing crimes and wrongdoings increase under the influence of drugs and alcohol. Anyone who breaks this precept is considered to have dishonored all of the precepts, because the ease of breaking each precept is increased with the consumption of drugs and drink. This precept concerns the respect one should have for their own mental health. Under drugs and alcohol, one is relinquishing the control over their mind. A present mind is required to reach enlightenment.

# Chapter Eleven: Buddhist Beliefs

There are many words that have been mentioned in this book that I have yet to explain. Many of them are Buddhist beliefs, like nirvana and karma. These will be explored in detail in this chapter. Many words common to Buddhism have more than one definition when translated, which makes a simple understanding almost impossible.

## Three Jewels/Three Refuges

To become a Buddhist, you must take refuge in the three jewels of Buddhism. These jewels are the Buddha, the Dharma, and the Sangha. There is a formal ceremony for this purpose performed at nearly all Buddhist schools, but it is possible to take refuge by simply reciting, "I take refuge in the Buddha, I take refuge in the Dharma, I take refuge in the Sangha." The reciting must be sincere and full of commitment for this to be meaningful. In Theravada Buddhism, they view taking refuge as going through a doorway to enter the teachings of the Buddha. Zen Buddhism sees these as more a vow than a prayer, they also recite them slightly differently;

"I take refuge in the Buddha, and wish that all sentient beings understand the great way"

"I take refuge in the Dharma, amd wish that all sentient beings delve into enlightenment, gaining knowledge as vast as the ocean. "

I take refuge in the Sangha, and wish that all sentient beings join together in harmony, without obstruction."

These are not vows or prayers that will call upon a mystic force to aid you in your search for enlightenment. They are only a way into the philosophy, and a way to access the nature that is already within you.

The Buddha usually refers to the historical Buddha, Siddhartha Gautama. Taking refuge in the Buddha refers to both the historical Buddha and the broader meaning of the term. In Mahayana Buddhism, the term Buddha refers also to Buddha-nature, the nature of all things and can mean enlightenment itself, not just one who is enlightened.

The Dharma, like Buddha, is not a word that lends itself to definite definitions and translations. It can mean several things. It refers, of course, to the teachings of Buddha, and the law of karma, the cycle of life, death, and rebirth. It also can mean ethical rules and mental thoughts. In Theravada Buddhism, the word can mean the conditions under which something comes to exist. Mahayana Buddhism can be used to mean the manifestation of reality. Two levels of Dharma are understood. One level is the teachings of the Buddha and the other it the path of Buddhism.

The Sangha, like most other words in Buddhism, has many meanings and a lot of depth. The term is most often used to refer to the monastic orders and the institutions of Buddhism. It can also be used in a similar fashion to how Christians use the word "church." A Sangha can be a group of Buddhists, large or small, lay or monastic, who practice together. A Sangha can also refer to all those who practice Buddhism, everywhere. It is impossible to achieve enlightenment on your own. To be a part of a Sangha is to get support and give support to others. The importance of Sangha cannot be overestimated.

## Karma

Karma is a term often used in Western culture. Usually it is referring to the idea that you get back what you give. The more bad karma that you put out into the world, the worse your life is going to me. Karma in Buddhist teachings is not very different from this basic, westernized definition. Buddhist teachings define karma as how our past actions will impact our future. Modern teachings of Buddhism state that everything in our current life is a direct result of our actions from our past life. It appears as though earlier forms of Buddhism did not believe that karma influenced every action and thing in a person's life, that every life is still subject to the natural order.

Karma follows Buddhists past their life; bad actions in a past life (bad karma) will lead to bad things happening in their new reincarnation. Even the Buddha fell prey to bad karma when his cousin attempted to kill him by dropping a boulder on him. His cousin missed, but the boulder fell on the Buddha's foot. The Buddha said that this was because in a past life he attempted to kill his step-brother.

Buddhists will try to gain more good karma than bad in their lives, but the goal is not to just be reincarnated into the best possible life. They want to escape the cycle of life, death, and rebirth altogether. Karma means action, and it is precisely that. It is self-determined action, not fate or an external cosmic force. We are in control of our own fates. Our own actions influence our futures.

The Buddha's words on karma were, "I am the owner of my karma. I inherit my karma. I am born of my karma. I am related to my karma. I live supported by my karma. Whatever karma I create, whether good or evil, that I shall inherit."

## Samsara

Samsara is the process of life, death, and rebirth that has been mentioned many times in this book. Samsara is a Sanskrit word meaning "to cycle." It can also mean to go round. It means that you are stuck in a cycle until you reach nirvana. In Buddhist teachings, we are stuck in samsara, which can be understood as a state of greed, dissatisfaction, or selfishness until we find enlightenment, which frees us from samsara. Samsara is not a place, but a process. With the understanding of the term samsara, the Four Noble Truths can be translated as such:

1. We are creating our own samsara.
2. This is how we are creating samsara.
3. We can stop creating samsara.
4. The way to stop is by following the Eightfold Path.

## Nirvana

Yes, it was the name of a band, but we are talking about it in relation to Buddhist teachings. Nirvana is also not a place, despite popular belief. Western Christo-centric cultures have a hard time understanding nirvana without comparing it to Heaven. This comparison is entirely incorrect. Nirvana is freedom from the bonds that enslave us. It is freedom from samsara. Nirvana is a state of consciousness. Nirvana has not been defined clearly, as language fails to even begin to accurately describe the state of nirvana.

The Buddha described nirvana in terms of what it is not; "*There is, monks, that plane where there is neither extension, nor motion, nor the plane of infinite ether...nor that of neither-perception-nor-non-perception, neither this world nor another, neither the moon nor the sun. Here, monks, I say that there is no coming or going or remaining or deceasing or uprising, for this is itself without support, without continuance in samsara, without mental object—this is itself the end of suffering."*

Theravada Buddhism teaches that there are two different nirvanas. The first is known as nirvana with remainders. This is a living person or being that has reached enlightenment. They are still subject to the suffering of life, but are no longer bound to it. The second is parinibbana (nibbana is the Pali word for nirvana). This is complete nirvana, when the enlightened being dies.

Mahayana Buddhism teaches the Bodhisattva, which means that its followers are dedicated to helping others reach enlightenment. They will refuse nirvana in favor of staying in this life to help others reach nirvana.

# Chapter Twelve: Buddhist Texts

Sacred Buddhist texts are called Sutras. These contain the words and teachings of the Buddha. Aside from these, there are also a number of supplemental Buddhist texts. The Tripitaka or Pali Canon, Mahayana Sutras, and the Tibetan Book of the Dead are three important noncanonical Buddhist texts. The Pali Canon includes discourse of the Buddha, but also the teachings of his students.

## The Tripitaka

This is the earliest collection of Buddhist writings in existence. They were initially composed through the oral tradition, but by the third century, they had been written down. The first part of the Tripitatka is the Vinaya Pitaka. This focuses on discipline. This part set the guidelines and rules for nuns and monks in the Sangha. There are 227 regulations for monks and a few additional rules for nuns. The second part is the Sutra Pitaka, which speaks to discourse. This part has sermons and lessons that the Buddha gave. The final part is the Abhidharma Pitaka. This is about special teachings; it's basically a hodgepodge of texts, including stories and songs about the Buddha's past lives. This is the only canonically accepted text in Theravada Buddhism.

Mahayana Buddhism accepts the Tripitaka as sacred text, but adds to it over 2,000 more writings which are referred to as Sutras.

## The Avatamsaka Sutra

The Avatamsaka Sutra, also known as The Flower Garland Sutra or The Flower Ornament Sutra, is a collection of smaller sutras that speak to the idea that all beings reflect each other, but also the Universe.

## The Brahma Net

The Brahma Net is all about discipline and morality. In particular, it contains the Ten Bodhisattva Precepts, which are practiced by all nuns and monks.

## The Prajnaparamita Sutra

The Prajnaparamita Sutra is also known as the Perfection of Wisdom Sutra. These sutras are held in high regard in the Mahayana traditions. The Prajnaparamita Sutra is regarded as the informant of the bodhisattva.

## The Jewel Heap (Ratnakuta) Sutra

This is one of the oldest Mahayana teachings. It is said that this was one of the first things the Buddha taught after realizing enlightenment. The Jewel Heap is about the Middle Way.

## The Lotus Sutra

The Lotus Sutra is one of the most well-known and venerated of the Mahayana Sutras. This sutra expresses that all can become a Buddha and attain nirvana. It is so well known because it has the distinctive feature of using parables, such as:

The Burning House, in which a man must get his children who are distracted by playing to leave a burning house; The Prodigal Son, in which a poor, miserable man gradually learns that he is wealthier than he can imagine; The Phantom City, in which a man leads people on a long journey with many difficulties on the way, and gives them the illusion of a gorgeous city to keep them motivated; The Gem in the Jacket, in which a man has a gem that he sews on the inside of his friend's jacket and his friend lives in poverty, never knowing about the gem; The Gem in the King's Top-Knot, in which a king gives out many gifts, but keeps his best gift only for one exceptional person; and The Excellent Physician, in which a group of children are dying from poison but do not take medicine, despite the fact that their parent is a physician.

## The Mahaparinirvana Sutra

The Mahayana Mahaparinirvana Sutra is said to have been given by the Buddha the night before he died. The sutras are mostly about Buddha-nature.

There are hundreds of other sacred texts and sutras in the Buddhist tradition. Unlike other Buddhists, Zen Buddhists don't emphasize the sacred texts, they rely on koans to inform their meditation and break them free from the confines of logical thinking.

# Final Words

Buddhism is an interesting and deep topic to cover. It is also relatively and deceptively simple. I do not say this to diminish it at all. I'm sure scholars could write dissertations on only one aspect of the philosophy. When I say it is simple, I mean to say that it's teachings are laid out in a simple format. The Eightfold Path, the Four Noble Truths, the Three Universal Truths, the Three Jewels. They seem incredibly simple, but these teachings can each take years to decipher and truly understand their meanings and each of them contain multiple meanings within their true meaning.

This philosophy requires thought, concentration, and meditation. It also requires a community. One cannot realize enlightenment alone, a Sangha is required. Zen Buddhism is even more collaborative and requires a close student-teacher relationship in order to master the art of zazen. Buddhism requires you to rethink your very perception of the universe and even more difficult, your perception of yourself. It's an endlessly fascinating subject.

I encourage and urge you to begin to practice Buddhism. It is not something you can understand simply by reading about it, it must be experienced. Words failed the Buddha when trying to describe nirvana, and they continue to fail today. Modern language and translations can muddy the original meaning of Buddhist terminology and words. This makes it all the more imperative that you take the three refuges and begin your own path to enlightenment.

## Reviews and Feedback

**If you enjoyed this book, found issues or wanted to get in contact:**

If you appreciated the information provided in this book, please take a few moments to share your opinions and post a review.

I would be very grateful for you in your support if you found this book useful.

**Link to rate this book:**
A shortened link to the book is below for your convenience:

**www.wisefoxpub.com/ethrate**

**Feedback:**

If you have any feedback, found any errors in the book or just wanted to get in contact to say hi, please feel free to email us at: contact@wisefoxpub.com

Thank you for reading this book, I hope you have found the information useful in understanding this topic.

# Free Bonus Guides on Meditation and Mindfulness

Get 3 free bonus guides to help you incorporate meditation and mindfulness into every day.

### Guide 1: The Power of Meditation
Learn more about the power of meditation and how it can help you in your personal and professional life.

### Guide 2: Stress Less
A guide to help reduce stress at home and work with meditation and mindfulness

### Guide 3: The End to Multitasking:
Learn how to get more done each day by avoiding multi-tasking and being more focused. This is a practical guide for work or study that includes focus exercises to improve mindfulness and increase focus and concentration.

www.wisefoxbooks.com/mindfulguide

## Errors and Feedback

## Please Contact Us If You Find Any Errors

While every effort is taken to ensure the quality and accuracy of this book. Spelling, grammar and other errors are often missed in the early versions of publication.

We appreciate you contacting us first if you noticed any errors in this book before taking any other action. This allows us to quickly fix these errors before it negatively impacts the author.

If you find any issues or errors with this book, please contact us and we'll correct these as soon as possible.

Readers that notify us of errors will be invited to receive advance reader copies of future books published.

**Errors:** errors@wisefoxpub.com

## Feedback

For any general feedback about the book, please feel free to contact us at the email address below:

**Feedback:** feedback@wisefoxpub.com

Printed in Great Britain
by Amazon